MINDSET DISCIPLINE SUCCESS

THE POWER OF YOUR MINDSET IN ACHIEVING
SUCCESS.

ETIENNE NAUDÉ

Cover Photo by::
Alec Jackson

TABLE OF CONTENTS

INTRODUCTION

Everyone Dreams of being successful in life.
Whether it's to achieve financial security, or improve interpersonal
relationships with friends, family or colleagues, success is a common
objective. But the path to being successful is rarely easy. A
combination of a positive mindset and discipline is needed to
overcome challenges, stay focused, and achieve your goals.

In this book, we will look at how discipline and a positive outlook are
essential for success. We'll go into detail about how important it is to
establish a growth mentality, reject restrictive ideas, and think
positively. We'll also discuss how to cultivate discipline, how to
establish consistent routines, and how to stop putting things off.

In the final chapter of the book, we'll talk about what success really
means and how to define it for yourself. We'll go over setting
reachable goals, overcoming obstacles and creating a success strategy.
Whether you're starting a new business, pursuing a hobby, or just want
to improve your personal life, this book will give you the methods and
strategies you need to succeed through thinking and discipline. Let's
start you on your pathway to success.

Chapter 1
Understanding Mindset

One of the most important things in obtaining success is the right mindset. Your mindset is the collection of ideas and opinions you have about the people and the world in general. Your capacity to accomplish your goals might be aided or hampered by your preconceived ideas and attitude.

We will discuss the idea of mindset and how it relates to achievement in this chapter. In this lesson, you will learn how to recognize your present thinking, the distinction between a fixed and growth mindset, and how to develop a growth mindset.

Growth versus Fixed Mindset

Understanding the distinction between a fixed and a growth mentality is the first step in understanding mindset. People who have a fixed mindset think that their skills and intelligence are unchangeable fixed traits. They frequently avoid taking chances or attempting new things because they perceive failure as a reflection of their competence.

People who have a growth mindset, on the other hand, know that they can improve their skills and intelligence through effort, tenacity, and dedication. They are more likely to take chances and attempt new things because they see failure as an opportunity to learn and grow.

According to research, people with a growth mentality have a higher chance of succeeding than those with a fixed perspective. The reason for this is because they look at problems with curiosity and an openness to learning. It also aids in overcoming disappointments and maintaining motivation in the face of difficulties.

It's crucial to first recognize your existing attitude before you can begin to create a growth mindset. The following questions can help you assess whether you have a fixed or growing mindset:

- Do you think your IQ and skills can be improved by effort and commitment, or do you think they are predetermined?
- Do you view risks and challenges as opportunities to learn and grow, or do you avoid them?
- Do you consider failure to be a reflection of your abilities or as an opportunity to grow and learn?
- When presented with challenges, do you easily give up or do you persevere and find a solution?
- Do you actively seek out constructive criticism and feedback, or do you avoid it?

If you've just realized that you have a fixed mindset, please don't worry; you can change that. Here are some tactics that could be useful:

You can learn more about your present mentality and the areas where you might need to make some changes by taking the following actions.

1. Embrace Challenges: Accept challenges as chances to learn and develop rather than avoiding them. Be curious and open to trying new things when you approach issues.

2. Look at Failure as an Opportunity: Instead of viewing failure as a reflection of your character, look at it as a chance to grow. Consider what went wrong and how you might improve going forward.

3. Develop Self-Compassion: Be compassionate with yourself when you fail or encounter difficulties. You should have compassion and empathy for yourself just as you would for a friend.

4. Take Advice from Feedback: Look for advice and helpful criticism from others. Take this criticism as a chance to grow and learn.

5. Focus on Effort: Focus more on the effort you put forth in order to accomplish your goals rather than just the results. Realize that work is a key factor in success.

By implementing these techniques, you can start to develop a development mindset and get rid of any limiting beliefs that you might have.

Conclusion

This chapter has examined the idea of mentality and how it relates to success. The difference between a fixed and growth mindset, how to recognize your current thinking, and how to develop a growth mindset have all been covered.

Keep in mind that mindset is not something that is fixed. It's a flexible idea that can evolve with time and effort. You can increase your success rate, expose yourself to new opportunities, and master new abilities by developing a growth mindset.

Chapter 2
Developing a Growth Mindset

We talked about the value of developing a growth mindset in the last chapter and how doing so could improve joy and accomplishment in life. We are going to talk about a few specific methods and techniques to develop a growth mindset as well as go further into the concept of a growth mindset in this chapter.

A growth attitude is described as follows. A growth mindset is simply a belief that, with work and practice, your knowledge and abilities can be developed and improved dramatically. This differs from a fixed mindset, that has an assumption that your abilities and skills are unchangeable and permanent.

The good news is that having a growth mindset is a quality that can be mastered. With work and repetition, you can strengthen and develop this mindset. Here are some tips and approaches for developing a growth mindset:

1. Face challenges head-on

Being able to see challenges as opportunities for development and learning is one of the traits of individuals with a growth mindset. They look for challenges and see them as opportunities to learn new skills and abilities rather than trying to avoid them. Try to adopt this mentality whenever you are faced with an impossible task or situation. Focus on the chance for progress and growth rather than the possibility of failure. Keep in mind that every challenge presents an opportunity to grow and learn.

2. Develop a passion for learning

People who have a growth mindset typically enjoy learning and push themselves to constantly improve and learn new things. They are constantly seeking out new information and experiences because they consider learning an endless process. Try to enjoy the joy of learning in order to cultivate a mindset of growth. Always look for possibilities for growth and new experiences, and approach them with an open mind and an eagerness to learn.

It doesn't matter if it's through a traditional education or independent research, make learning a priority in your life.

3. Focus on effort rather than talent

People who have a growth mindset often place more value on effort than talent. They understand that success is the result of endurance and hard work rather than natural talent. Try to embrace this similar emphasis on effort over talent if you want to build a growth mindset. Focus on the time and energy you invested in honing your skills and abilities rather than your natural ability. Recognize that effort and practice, rather than talent, is what lead to success.

4. Accept failure.

Failure is seen as a natural part of learning by those with a growth mindset. They understand that failing is not a reason to give up but rather a chance to grow and learn. Try to adopt the same attitude toward failure in order to establish a growth mentality. Instead of viewing failure as a sign of weakness or incompetence, embrace it as an opportunity to learn and grow. Understand that failure is an essential part of learning and that each failure moves you one step closer to success.

5. Surround yourself with uplifting people

Finally, surround yourself with people who will help and support you in developing a growth mentality. Look for mentors and role models that are growth-minded, and stay away from people who negatively impact your efforts to develop this mindset.

By applying these methods and ideas, you will begin to develop a growth mindset, which will help you experience higher levels of satisfaction and achievement in every aspect of your life.

Having a development mindset requires constant practice and effort, but the benefits are well worth the trouble. You can develop a mindset that will enable you to reach your greatest potential and lead a life of meaning and fulfillment.

Chapter 3
Overcoming Limiting Beliefs

We talked about the value of having a growth mindset in the last chapter and how it can increase the quality of your life. Although many of us are etching closer towards acquiring a growth mindset, many of us still have limiting beliefs that prevent us from achieving our full potential.

We all have limiting attitudes and beliefs about our potential, capabilities, and ourselves. They may be deeply ingrained and be the result of prior experiences or insecurities within ourselves.

The good news is that limiting beliefs are not permanent or unchangeable. With effort and practice, we can learn to recognize and overcome these beliefs and develop a more positive and empowering mindset. Here are some strategies and techniques for overcoming your limiting beliefs:

1. Identify your limiting beliefs

The first step in overcoming limiting beliefs is to identify them. This can be challenging, as limiting beliefs are often deeply ingrained and may be difficult to recognize. However, by paying attention to your thoughts, actions and feelings, you can begin to identify patterns of negative thinking and beliefs that may be holding you back.

Take some time and think about how you perceive yourself, your potential, and your skills. Write them down and examine them thoroughly. Are they founded on assumptions rather than on facts and evidence? Are they encouraging and empowering, or do they hinder your growth and potential?

2. Examine your limiting assumptions

The next stage is to confront the limiting opinions you have about yourself. Look for evidence to disprove your negative beliefs about yourself, then replace them with more empowering and uplifting ones.

For instance, if you have a limiting thought that prevents you from achieving your goals, you can disprove it by reminding yourself of your past achievements and successes. Instead of concentrating on your perceived weaknesses, look for evidence of your skills and capabilities.

3. Change self-defeating language

Self-doubt usually manifests in the form of negative self-talk. We frequently speak negatively and harshly to ourselves, which can support our limiting beliefs and prevent us from reaching our full potential.

To overcome negative self-talk, try to reframe your thoughts in more positive and empowering ways. Instead of saying "I can't do this," try saying "I can do this if I put in the effort and practice." Instead of focusing on your perceived weaknesses, focus on your strengths and abilities.

4. Take action

One of the most effective ways to overcome self-doubt is to take action towards your goals. By taking action, you have already taken the first step and therein demonstrate to yourself that you are capable of achieving your goals and that fear of failure, self-doubt, and limiting beliefs are holding you back.

Start by setting small, achievable goals that align with your values and goals. Take action towards these goals, even if it feels uncomfortable. Most importantly, celebrate your successes and use them as evidence to challenge your limiting beliefs.

5. Seek support

Finally, seek support from others who can help you overcome your self-doubt and limiting beliefs. This may include friends, family members, mentors, or a professional therapist or coach, depending on your circumstances and relationships with the aforementioned. Choose wisely.

Seek advice and feedback from those who have overcome similar challenges, and look for opportunities to learn and grow from their experiences.

By adopting these strategies and techniques, you can begin to overcome your self-doubt and develop a more positive and empowering mindset. Remember, overcoming limiting beliefs is a process that requires consistent effort and practice, but the rewards are well worth the effort. With time and dedication, you can cultivate a mindset that will help you achieve your full potential and live the life you deserve, a life of purpose and fulfillment.

Chapter 4
What is Discipline?

Discipline is often seen as a negative concept - something that is associated with punishment and strict rules. However, when it comes to achieving success, discipline is a vital component. In this chapter, we will explore what discipline is, why it is important, and how you can develop discipline in your own life.

At its core, discipline is the ability to control your behavior and take action even when you don't feel like it. It involves making a commitment to your goals and taking consistent action towards them, even when it's difficult or uncomfortable. Discipline is not about perfection or strict adherence to rules, but rather it's about making intentional choices that align with your values and goals.

Discipline is important because it allows you to stay focused on your goals and make progress towards them, even in the face of obstacles or distractions. It helps you build habits and routines that support your goals, and it gives you the strength and resilience to push through challenges and setbacks.

One of the keys to developing discipline is to set clear and specific goals. When you have a clear idea of what you want to achieve, you can then create a plan of action and take steps towards achieving your goals. It's also important to break your goals down into smaller, more manageable tasks. This helps you avoid feeling overwhelmed and makes it easier to stay focused and motivated.

Another important aspect of developing discipline is to establish habits and routines that support your goals. Habits are powerful because they become automatic over time, making it easier to take action even when you don't feel like it. To establish new habits, start small and focus on consistency. For example, if your goal is to exercise every day, start by committing to 10 minutes of exercise each day and gradually increase the duration over time.

Discipline also involves learning to manage your time effectively. Time is a finite resource, and it's important to use it wisely if you want to achieve your goals. One way to manage your time effectively is to create a schedule or routine that supports your goals. This can involve setting aside dedicated time each day for specific tasks or activities, or it can involve batching similar tasks together to increase efficiency.

Finally, discipline requires self-control and self-regulation. This involves being aware of your thoughts, emotions, and impulses, and learning to manage them effectively. One way to develop self-control is to practice mindfulness. Mindfulness involves paying attention to the present moment without judgment. It can help you develop greater self-awareness and make intentional choices that support your goals.

In conclusion, discipline is a vital component of achieving success. By setting clear and specific goals, establishing habits and routines that support your goals, managing your time effectively, developing a growth mindset, and practicing self-control and self-regulation, you can develop the discipline you need to achieve your goals. Remember, discipline is not about perfection or strict adherence to rules, but rather it's about making intentional choices that align with your values and goals. With practice and perseverance, you can develop the discipline you need to achieve the success you desire.

Chapter 5
Cultivating Discipline for Success

One of the most important traits of a successful person is typically thought to be discipline. It is the ability to commit to a goal and complete it, despite difficulty or the need for sacrifice. Discipline is a learned characteristic that can be developed over time with patience.

In this chapter we will discuss Discipline and how it directly ties to success. We'll also go through methods for gaining self-control and creating routines that will help you achieve your objectives.

What is Discipline?

The ability to control your desires, emotions, and behaviors when trying to achieve your goal is commonly referred to as discipline. It involves setting goals, developing a plan, and consistently following through on your action plan over time. High levels of mindfulness, self-control, and determination are essential for discipline.

Discipline is directly linked to sacrifice and delayed gratification. In order to accomplish long-term goals, it means saying "no" to temporary pleasures. For example, a disciplined person can decide against going out with friends so they can focus on studying or working on a project. They are aware that their present choices will affect how successful they are in the future.

Why is Discipline Important for Success?

Success demands discipline for a number of reasons. The first benefit is that it enables you to maintain focus on your goals and move steadily closer to achieving them. Without self-control, it is easy to get sidetracked by other responsibilities or to put off from doing something crucial.

Secondly, discipline helps in developing habits that help you achieve your goals. By consistently pursuing your goals, you form habits that make it easier to carry out that behavior over time. By automating these behaviors, you can easily stay on track and accomplish your goals.

Thirdly, discipline creates endurance, which helps in overcoming challenges. Discipline enables you to stay focused on your goals and take action to get over obstacles when you face challenges or setbacks. It enables you to stay motivated and succeed in the face of adversity.

How to Develop Self-Discipline

Self-discipline development is a process that takes time, effort, and dedication. It involves establishing routines that help you achieve your goals and developing impulse and emotional control. Here are some methods to improve self-control:

1. Set specific goals. You need to have a firm understanding of your goals in order to develop discipline. Create measurable goals that are in line with your values and primary goals.

2. Develop a plan: After you've decided on your goals, establish a plan of action for accomplishing them. Create a timetable for achieving each step in your goals by breaking them down into smaller, more doable steps.

3. Eliminate any distractions that could make it harder for you to stay focused on your objectives. This might refer to email, social media, or other electronic devices. Use these distractions moderately or get rid of them altogether.

4. Establish a routine: Create a schedule that supports your goals and keeps you on track. This can involve designating certain hours for work, physical activity, or other hobbies.

5. Engage in mindfulness exercises: Mindfulness is the discipline of paying attention to the present moment and your current task. You'll be able to maintain focus while staying out of trouble.

6. Talk to yourself positively: Talking to yourself positively is a powerful way to motivate yourself. Use encouraging statements to remind yourself of your goals and maintain motivation rather than concentrating on negative thoughts or self-doubt.

Chapter 6
Creating Habits for Success

We all have daily habits, whether they are constructive or destructive. Routines that we perform instinctively and without much thought are called habits. Good habits are crucial to success because they enable us to establish a routine and structure that will help us achieve our goals. This chapter will cover the importance of developing productive habits as well as practical methods for doing so.

Why are Habits Important for Success?

Because they give us a sense of structure and forward motion, habits are vital to success. We are less likely to getting sidetracked or putting things off when we follow a fixed pattern. Instead, we are more inclined to maintain our focus on our goals and make steady progress toward achieving them.

Developing healthy habits also aids in the development of self-control and discipline. In essence, when we commit to a habit, we are committing to a behavior that will assist us in achieving our goals. By repeatedly engaging in this action, we cultivate self-control and discipline, two traits that are essential to success.

How to Create Habits for Success

Creating habits for success involves a few key steps.

1. Identify the Habit

Identifying what specific actions you would like to adopt is the first step in developing a habit for success. You should act in a way that will enable you to accomplish your goals. For example, if you want to publish a book, it would be an excellent habit to write for an hour every day. 2. Start Small

It's crucial to start small and build your way up when developing a habit. A new behavior all at once might be difficult and overwhelming to stick to. Start instead with a reasonable, doable goal

For example, if you want to start working out every day, start by working out for ten minutes every day.

3. Be Consistent

When it comes to forming habits, consistency is essential. You should try to put your new behavior into practice every day, ideally at the same time. It will be simpler for you to establish the habit as a routine if you are consistent.

4. Track Your Progress

Tracking your progress will keep you motivated and on course. You can accomplish this by using a habit tracker, a straightforward application that enables you to log your daily progress. You can see how far you've come and how much closer you are to accomplishing your goals by keeping track of your progress.

5. Hold Yourself Accountable

Holding yourself responsible for your new habit is important, as well. This can be done by committing to yourself or by telling someone else what your goal is. You'll be more likely to persist with your habit and reach your goals if you hold yourself accountable.

Conclusion

Developing successful habits is vital for achieving the goals you have set. You can gain momentum, cultivate discipline, and maintain focus on what you want to achieve by incorporating new behaviors into your daily routine. Start out modest, maintain consistency, monitor your advancement, and keep yourself accountable. You can develop habits using these techniques that will help you succeed in all aspects of your life.

Chapter 7
Overcoming Procrastination

Procrastination is a widespread issue that a lot of people struggle with, and it can have a negative impact on performance and productivity. Delaying or postponing tasks is known as procrastination, and it frequently results in stress, anxiety, and missed deadlines. We will cover methods for overcoming procrastination and boosting productivity in this chapter.

1. Identify the Reasons for Procrastination

Understanding exactly why you delay things is the first step in conquering procrastination. Procrastination can be triggered by a number of things, including overwhelm, lack of motivation, and fear of failure. You can develop strategies for dealing with your procrastination by identifying its underlying causes.

2. Break Down Tasks into Smaller Chunks

To combat procrastination, it may be helpful to divide big tasks into smaller, more manageable tasks. It can be simple to delay and put off an assignment that looks overwhelming. Making the task feel more manageable and less overwhelming is possible by breaking it up into smaller components. You can feel progress and accomplishment as you complete each small step by breaking down a difficult task.

3. Use a Timer

Procrastination can be avoided with the use of a timer. Set a timer for a certain duration, for example 25 minutes, and focus solely on the task at hand until the alarm sounds. The Pomodoro Technique is a method that helps keep you focused and productive. Take a brief pause once the timer sounds before beginning another work session.

4. Create a Schedule

Another successful strategy for overcoming procrastination is to make a schedule or to-do list. Make a list of all the tasks that you need to perform and arrange them in order of importance.

Create a schedule for when you will work on each task, and give each one a deadline. You can stay focused and motivated to complete each activity by having a clear plan.

5. Eliminate Distractions

One of the most common causes people put things off is distractions. Eliminating distractions and creating a productive environment is key to conquering procrastination. Social networking, email, and phone notifications are a few examples of typical distractions. To assist you keep focused on the task at hand, turn off the notifications on your phone, close the social media and email tabs, and make a quiet environment.

6. Get an Accountability Partner

Procrastination can be defeated with the help of an accountability partner. Identify an associate who can hold you accountable for completing assignments on time. Together, you should make a plan for how you will work together to achieve your goals after sharing them with your accountability partner. Being motivated and overcoming procrastination might be aided by being aware that someone else is depending on you.

7. Reward Yourself

A strong motivator for overcoming procrastination is rewarding oneself. After completing a task, give yourself a reward by taking a break, going for a stroll, or watching an episode of your favourite tv series. You can boost your sense of achievement and drive to keep working toward your goals by rewarding yourself as you finish tasks.

Chapter 8
Defining Success

Success can mean a variety of things to different people. It's an idea that is defined by a person's individual viewpoints, principles, and aspirations. For some, it may mean becoming financially independent, while for others, it might mean rising to the top of their career or having a significant impact on society. In this chapter, we'll look at the various definitions of success and the different elements that go into achieving it.

Defining Success

The achievement of specific goals or benchmarks is often associated with success. However, success is a journey as much as a destination, and that needs to be understood. The act of pursuing a goal and moving forward is what makes us feel satisfied and accomplished. It's important to define success in a way that is relevant to your life as a whole.

Identifying your basic values and aligning them with your goals is one approach to achieving success. Values serve as the compass that directs our actions, choices, and attitudes. We are more driven and dedicated to reaching our goals when they are consistent with our values. For instance, if honesty and integrity are among your primary beliefs, you might view success as attaining your objectives in a moral and open way.

Putting an emphasis on your own development and growth is another way to define success. Success can be defined as the pursuit of ongoing learning, personal growth, and improvement. We can learn new abilities and skills that assist us in growing as individuals when we set goals that challenge us and take us outside of our comfort zones. Success in this sense is more about the process of learning and developing than it is about reaching a particular result.

Factors Contributing to Success

While individual goals and values ultimately determine success, there are a few things that are frequently linked to achieving it. These consist of:

1. Motivation: Our drive to achieve our goals comes from motivation. We remain focused and motivated in the face of difficulties and hurdles because of our inner will to succeed.

2. Persistence: The ability to keep going even in the face of failure and setbacks is persistence. It is the determination to attempt something repeatedly and to accept lessons from failures and mistakes.

3. Self-control: Self-control is the ability to keep our focused attention and dedication to our goals in the face of temptations and distractions. Self-control and self-regulation exercises are what keep us on track.

4. Resilience: Being able to endure problems and come out stronger from adversity is resilience. It is the ability to adapt to change despite challenging situations.

5. Social support: Those close to us who encourage, direct, and help us achieve our objectives are referred to as social support. Having a solid support system can keep us driven and responsible.

Conclusion

There are several aspects to success, and it has many distinct definitions. It's important to understand that success includes the process of learning and growth as well as the accomplishment of specific goals or milestones. We become more motivated and dedicated to obtaining it when we define success in a way that is meaningful and applicable to our lives.

We can maintain our dedication to our goals by relying on the success-enhancing factors including motivation, perseverance, discipline, resilience, and social support. The importance of goal-setting and planning for achievement will be discussed in more detail in the next chapter.

Chapter 9
Setting Goals and Planning for Success

In addition to maintaining a positive outlook and self-control, success also involves setting and achieving goals. Goals provide us with focus and direction, as well as a way to track our development. However, setting goals can be hard, and many people have trouble achieving them. In this chapter, we will discuss the importance of goal setting and provide helpful suggestions for setting and achieving your goals.

The Importance of Setting Goals

Goal setting is a crucial component of success because it helps us clarify what we want to achieve and provides a roadmap for getting there. Goals give us direction and purpose, help us focus our time and energy, and motivate us to take action. Without goals, we can feel lost, unmotivated, and unsure of where to direct our efforts.

Setting goals also enables us to monitor our development and growth. We can monitor our progress and evaluate our achievements by creating clear, achievable objectives. This can be greatly motivating and inspire us to persevere even in the face of obstacles.

Obstacles to Setting Goals

Even though setting goals is important, many people find it challenging to do so. The following are some common obstacles to developing goals:

1. A lack of clarity: Setting clear goals is difficult if you don't know what you want to accomplish. It can be challenging to know where to begin when there is a lack of clarity, which can result in confusion and indecision.

2. Fear of failure: Setting goals can be intimidating since it requires taking a chance on failure and putting yourself out there. Setting challenging objectives and acting on them can both be difficult when you are afraid of failing.

3. Procrastination: Avoid procrastination at all costs because it undermines goal-setting. Setting goals or taking action towards them can be difficult, especially if they are challenging or involve a lot of effort.

4. Lack of motivation: It can be hard to stay motivated and focused, even when you are aware of what you want to do. Lack of motivation can make it challenging to set objectives and difficult to achieve them.

Tips for Setting Goals
Here are some tips for setting and achieving your goals:

1. Start with why: Think about your values and what drives you before you begin to develop goals. It can be simpler to stay motivated if you have a clear idea of why you want to do something.

2. Make sure your objectives are SMART: specific, measurable, achievable, timely, and relevant. You can specify what you want to accomplish and design a path to get there by making your goals SMART.

3. Break big goals into smaller steps: Since big goals can be intimidating, it is wise to divide them into smaller, easier-to-achieve steps. This can help take action toward your goals while providing you with a sense of progress and achievement along the way.

4. Visualize success: Success visualization is a potent motivator. Think about how it will feel when you accomplish your goals and use that as motivation to keep going.

Conclusion
A crucial element of success is setting and achieving goals. You can accomplish big things if you make precise, measurable goals, divide them into smaller steps, and maintain motivation and accountability.

Always keep in mind that setting goals is a continuous process. Review your goals frequently, revise as necessary, and acknowledge your accomplishments as you go.

Chapter 10
Overcoming Obstacles and Challenges

No matter how well we plan or how dedicated we are to reaching our goals, we are bound to stumble across obstacles and setbacks. These challenges could be internal, like self-doubt or a fear of failing, or external, such as sudden changes in our circumstances or failures at work. It's crucial to keep in mind that these challenges aren't barriers to our success, but rather chances for development and education.

Reframe Your Mindset

Reframing the way we think is the first step in conquering obstacles and challenges. We might choose to view challenges as chances for improvement and growth rather than as insurmountable barriers. This means shifting our focus from the problem to the solution, and from the negative to the positive. For example, "What can I learn from this experience?" or "How can I use this challenge to become stronger?" are encouraging questions we can ask ourselves to help reframe our mindset.

Take Action

Once we've reframed our mindset, the next step is to take action. That means breaking down our goals into smaller, manageable steps and taking consistent, focused action towards them. We can also look for support and guidance from others who have faced similar challenges and overcome them. However, it's important to be cautious about who we trust.

Build Resilience

The secret to overcoming obstacles and challenges is to cultivate resilience. Resilience is the ability to bounce back from setbacks and continue toward the goals we have set. We can prioritize self-care and self-compassion, look for opportunities for learning and growth, and build a strong support system of friends, family, and mentors to increase our resilience.

Always keep in mind that setting goals is a continuous process. Review your goals frequently, revise as necessary, and acknowledge your accomplishments as you go.

Stay Focused on Your Goal

The final thing to remember is to keep our eyes on the prize. We must continue to focus on our vision while upholding our principles and values. This can be accomplished by regularly assessing our performance, making necessary changes to our plans, and reminding ourselves of the benefits of achieving our goals.

Ultimately, overcoming problems and hurdles is an important step on the road to success. We can use these difficulties as a springboard for learning and development, and ultimately achieve our intended results by shifting our perspective, taking action, cultivating resilience, and remaining goal-focused.

Chapter 11
Celebrating your Successes

Celebrating your successes is one of the most crucial elements of success. Celebrating your achievements will boost your belief in yourself while also giving you a chance to reflect and evolve. This chapter will discuss the value of celebrating your accomplishments as well as some effective methods.

Why Celebrating Your Successes Is Important

For a number of reasons, it's crucial to recognize your accomplishments. It first assists you in recognizing and appreciating how you've grown. It is easy to become buried in daily tasks and lose sight of your accomplishments. Taking time to celebrate your victories offers you an opportunity to think back on your journey and acknowledge the hard work you have put in.

Secondly, recognizing your accomplishments might inspire you and increase your self-assurance. Your momentum might increase and your sense of accomplishment can spread to other aspects of your life as a result of successes. By recognizing your accomplishments, you may build a constructive feedback system that will encourage further growth.

Thirdly, celebrating your accomplishments offers a chance to learn. When you take the time to acknowledge your accomplishments, you have the opportunity to consider what worked and what didn't. This might assist you in differentiating between techniques that worked and those that didn't. You can learn lessons from your triumphs that will help you be more successful in the future.

How to Celebrate Your Successes

There are many ways to recognize your accomplishments. The secret is to discover a path that resonates with you and is consistent with what you stand for and what you want. Here are some suggestions to get you going:

1. Recognize Your Success: Take time to reflect on your accomplishments. Your accomplishments should be noted down, discussed with someone, or given some thought.

2. Treat Yourself: Do something you enjoy or have been wanting to do for yourself. It might be as straightforward as a new book or a favorite cuisine. It's crucial to recognize your accomplishments in a way that means something to you.

3. Celebrate with Others: Rejoice in your accomplishments alongside others who have helped you along the way. This might include close relatives, friends, or coworkers. Celebrating with others can make you feel connected and supported and is a good opportunity to express gratitude to those who have assisted you in achieving your objectives.

4. Reflect and Learn: Give yourself some time to think back on your accomplishments and determine what worked and what didn't. Make use of this knowledge to guide your future work and enhance your strategy.

Conclusion

A key component of success is recognizing and appreciating your accomplishments. You may improve your future efforts and increase your drive and confidence by taking the time to think on what went well, reward yourself, and recognize your accomplishments. Don't forget to develop a means to recognize your accomplishments that is consistent with your values and aims, and don't be shy about telling others about them.